I belie[...] in Allah

Written by **Bachar Karroum**

Illustrated by Luis Peres

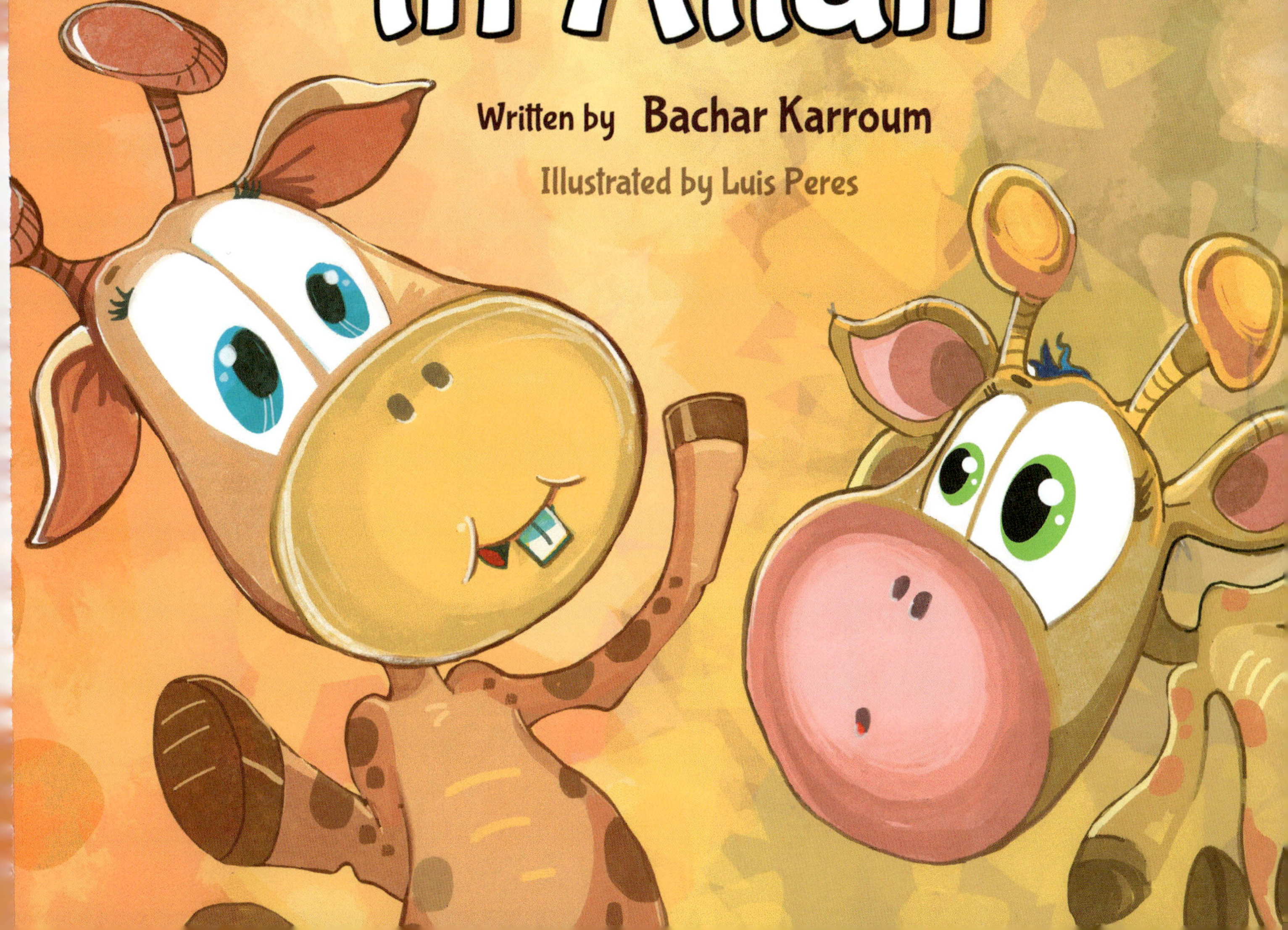

This book is inspired by the short story written by Pablo J.Luis Molinero about two babies within their mother's womb wondering whether mother exists or not and whether there's any life after birth.

ISBN : 978 1 988779 26 3
Author : Bachar Karroum
Illustrator : Luis Peres (www.icreateworlds.net)
Editor : Tamara Rittershaus, Aline Massouh
Proofreader : Christina Cutting

This book belongs to:

Ali and Sami are spending
the day at the park with their moms.
Sami raced across the playground
to his friend.

"Hey Ali, my mommy will have a baby! A baby girl!"

"So exciting! Allah is giving you a baby sister, just like He gave me a baby brother!"

"Allah? Do you actually believe in Allah?" asked Sami.

"Of course, I do, don't you?"
answered Ali.

"Hmm...how can I believe in someone I can 't even see?" questioned Sami.

Ali, surprised by
Sami 's answer, had an idea.
"Can I tell you a story?"

"Sure, I like stories!" said Sami.

A mommy giraffe once had TWO babies in her belly—Kiki and Gigi.

One day, feeling the presence
of someone beside her,
Kiki asked her sister,
"Do you know what we're doing here?"

Surprised by the voice,
Gigi instantly replied,
"hmm . . . maybe we are
here to get ready to go
to another place."

Shaking her head,
Kiki exclaimed,
"Total nonsense!
How can you even
imagine a place
different from here?"

"I just feel it," replied Gigi. "Maybe we won't float around anymore. I really can't wait to see what our future brings."

"That is silly," replied Kiki. "Our umbilical cord provides us with food and everything we need! We can 't move too far from it."

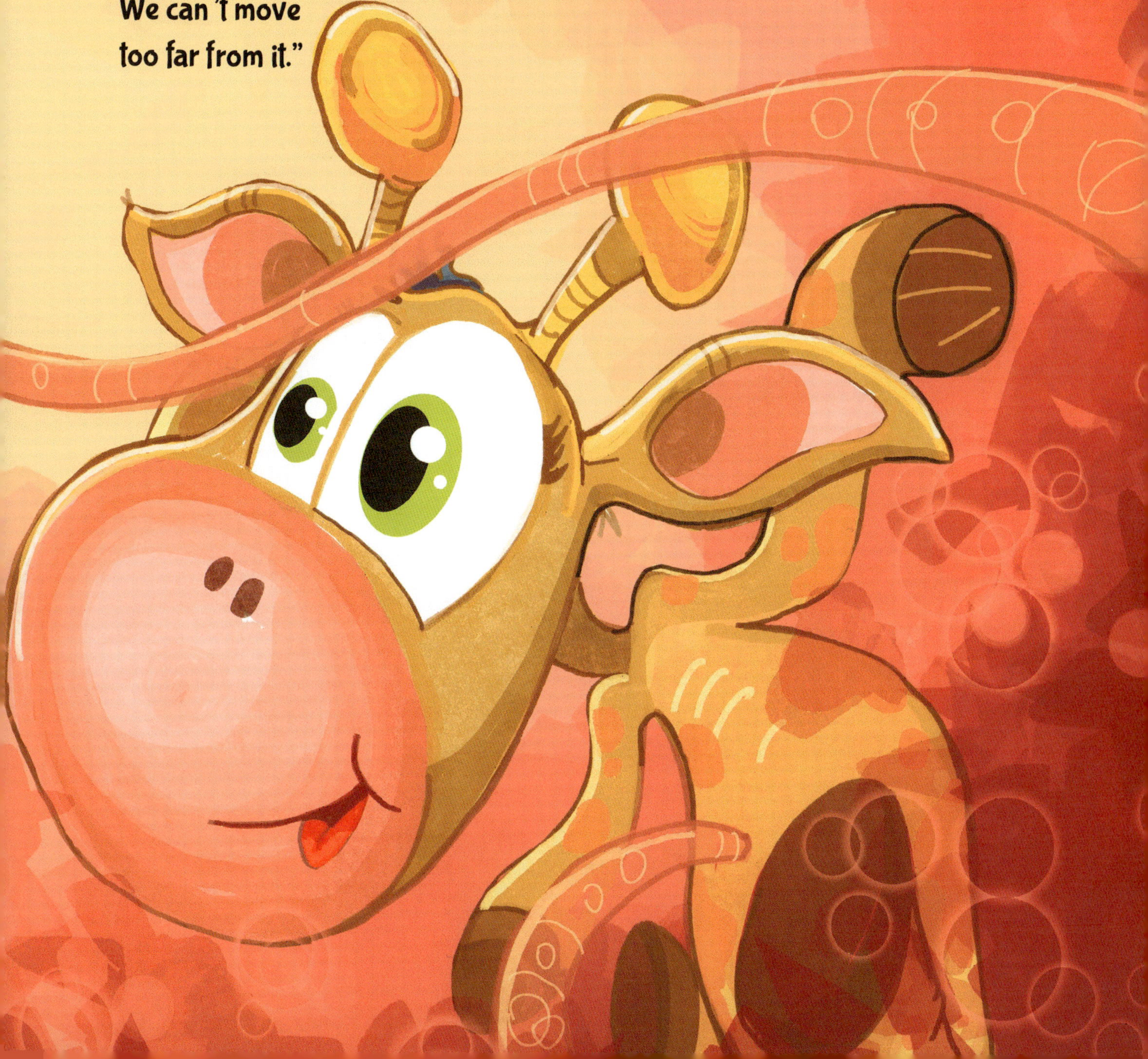

"What if there was another way, and
we didn't need our cords anymore?
Can you imagine it just for a minute?"
Gigi asked.

"I 'm sorry, sister," said Kiki.
"If there were another place, others would have come back to tell us.
Besides, we wouldn 't know what to
do in a different place."

"Well," said Gigi, "what if Mother took care of us and helped us live in the new world?"

"Mother?!
You actually believe
in Mother?" exclaimed Kiki.
"How do you know she exists;
you can 't even see her!"

"Mother is all around us," explained Gigi. "Without her, this place could not exist and neither could we."

"Well, I can't see her," said Kiki.
"So, I can't believe in her."

"Sometimes, when you're quiet and listen closely,
you can hear mother's loving voice calling down from above.
I believe mother is there waiting for us to give us all her love,"
Gigi whispered.

"That was interesting, Ali.
I never thought about it that way.

Neither giraffe could see their mother from inside,
but one of them had faith that she existed.

I understand it's the same for Allah, we can't see Him,
but we believe in Him and we believe He exists...

I can't wait
to meet my little sister,
and one day,
tell her the story Inchallah!"